To request permission, contact the publisher at du.tsu@sacredas123.com

Paperback: ISBN 979-8-9893756-0-8
Ebook: ISBN: 979-8-9893756-1-5

Library of Congress Number: 2023921981

Prepared for Publication by Hyperspace Internet Technologies, Inc.
The photographs are from the author's personal library and the illustrations
are graphically enhanced versions of the author's hand drawn originals.

Published by
Elizabeth M. Richie

Dedication

I dedicate **Homespun: A Return to the Land** to Larry Richie without whom this wonderful story could not have unfolded with so much music, so many laughs and so much love!

And I dedicate it also to our two dear sons, Elijah and Isaiah, whom I had the privilege and absolute delight of Mothering on that beautiful West Virginia hillside!

Prologue

A Picture Speaks a Thousand Words!

Once upon a time, around 1977, two very good friends shared an idea. Well... not just an idea... a powerful, beautiful Vision!

On summer college break, one of the friends, named Betsy, visited relatives who lived in Washington state. They took her to see a "homestead" on a little inlet on the coast of British Columbia. A retired art professor had bought an idyllic forested property. He had managed to build a good-sized log house. He and his wife had a lovely garden. They had a canoe and a motorboat. They raised chickens. Their children ran free. It seemed, to the girl, like a dream come true. Indeed, going "Back to the Land" was all in fashion during the 1960's and 70's, and this was a perfect example.

Not long afterward, Betsy, who was a newspaper reporter, described the homestead to her friend, Larry, who was a high school teacher. Both believed it would be a wonderful thing to do together! They talked and dreamed about following the art professor's lead. They planned and saved their money. They pooled their cash and bought 54 acres for $13,000 in West Virginia. Quite a bargain indeed!

This **Homespun Picture Book** documents the first year of their activities on their "homestead". This consisted mainly of building a home out of a stone root cellar that had been built into the side of a hill. The old farmhouse that had stood in front of the root cellar had burned down before they bought the property, and the flames took the roof off the cellar along with the old house.

Betsy had a Grandmother named Pearl Ann, who lived alone in a nursing home and they corresponded almost daily. One Christmas, Betsy made this picture book for Pearl Ann.

(In the **Epilogue** you'll find a poem that Larry wrote for their wedding ceremony. It kinda says it all!)

So now, I will let the pictures speak....

**With Love and
good wishes, to
my grandmother
1980**

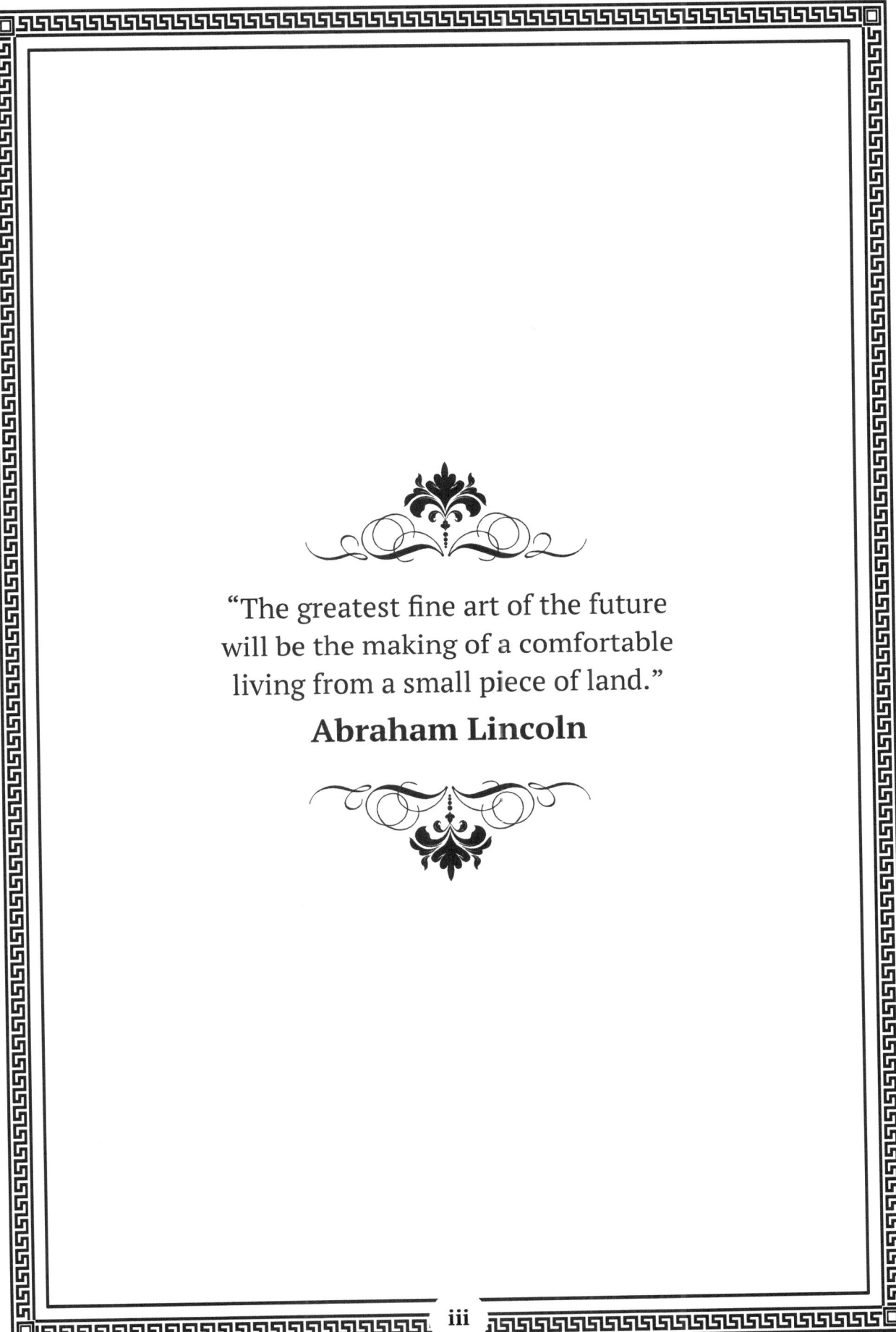

"The greatest fine art of the future will be the making of a comfortable living from a small piece of land."

Abraham Lincoln

Once upon a time,

when America was middle aged and modern, some people began to think that typical American living had lost its grace and charm. In the hustle of competitive business and massive industry, there was little reminder of nature's way of peace and beauty.

So, a second wave of American pioneers was born, commonly seeking to retune life to the harmonies of Mother Nature. Blending some of the new and some of the old, they began again.

Two of these pioneering spirits are Larry and Betsy. And here-in follows a homespun picture book showing their simple adventures and misadventures.

Where in America can people with only modest means find a place to "homestead," such as Betsy and Larry sought to do?

They had to find what is called "marginal land," so named because its just not the sort of place to build a factory, skyscaper or residential development.

Betsy and Larry found their land in West Virginia. "Mountainmen always free," the state motto, seemed to offer an omen. Freedom, after all, was an essential ingredient for their adventure.

On a warm June day they pulled their camper-trailer and light truck onto their $54^{9/16}$ acres on Elk Fork Road. It didn't look like this at first when they first arrived. Here, the Jungle-like brush has been cut from the fields.

But in the very beginning, they pitched camp in safari-like fashion. And sure enough, wild animals emerged from the bush, prowling about and stalking the invaders of their territory.

Betsy, ever energetic, immediately put new equipment to the test, particularly making certain that the lawn chairs could hold the weight she had gained through many months of inactivity behind a desk and typewriter.

The property's original latrine still stood, well ventilated and cock-eyed. Proximity to the road, however, spoiled the meditative calm sought with regularity therein.

Hey Ethel, take a gander up yonder! There's a fellow on the commode! Ha Ha Ha Ha

Larry, always the clever and resourceful scrounger, immediately proved his worth in the struggle for survival. For instance, an abandoned gas range, the ghastly, ghostly reminder of by gone residents was resurrected and converted to a wood burner. Presto! The first hot meal!

Meanwhile, Betsy began to master the illusive culinary art of peanut butter and jelly bread, a staple for the homesteaders.

A pit to trap wild game?

Phew! I ain't used to work

Most assuredly not.

The silly fact of the matter is,one of the first necessities of a homestead is an outhouse. And an outhouse requires a pit over which it is set.
Betsy picked while Larry bailed dirt. Team work prevailed.

Toiling under the sun, Betsy and Larry worked diligently to carve an existence from the untamed earth. A tiny, late garden was cultivated and fenced to protect it from their flock of chickens, and other "critters."

The only building on the land which was worth keeping was repaired and remodeled to provide a combination chicken coop, tool shed and car and motor cycle port.

And after a hard day's work, what could be more pleasurable than a shower from a barrel warmed by the sun?

Or what's more satisfying than the wealth of a homestead garden?

But winter was drawing nigh and soon the warmth of summer would give way to the chills of the North wind. Even as August passed, cool nights heralded the need for a more substantial shelter.

The answer to the shelter question was almost obvious. With a little imagination and alot of work the old root cellar would make a dandy home!

(That's Betsy leaning in the doorway. Leaning is one of her favorite positions.)

They turned to the forests for free lumber. Using a mammoth chain saw, Larry and Betsy worked against the clock to throw up a roof before the snows came.

Each board and beam was a challenge to the greenhorn lumberjacks. And muscles were asked to do the work of draft mules.

Every moment of exertion proved worthwhile,

as a little stone cottage became home.

And peanut butter and jelly tasted just
as good indoors as out.

The work never ceased, even in winter. Firewood was needed to warm the cottage and there had been no time for stocking up during the fall.

The tractor came from Pennsylvania, a gift of Larry's parents.

In March, when the sugar maple sap began to flow, the homesteaders spent many an hour outdoors boiling down the precious liquid into tasty syrup.

Sure enough, the first winter wound down, bringing with it a time for spring cleaning-burning brush and so much more to be done.

But as in the past, there was (and is) always time and reason for joy.

What could be more curious or amusing than a tree with a smoke-stack.

Time races onward.

But the homesteaders hope that-as in the proverbial race between the tortoise and the hare-the slower more peaceful pace will prevail.

Elizabeth Ritchie

The end of the beginning.

Epilogue

So, that was the Beginning.....1979...

We lived six great years in the root cellar, which we called "The Stone Cottage". It was/is 15 feet by 15 feet, (it's still standing), and it has a "loft" where we slept in an upper back corner. Underneath our bed loft was our storage

Find the Cottage, the Canteen, the Cat.

area for canned goods and other items. We had no electricity except for a car battery for a radio. We had no television or telephone. Of course, mobile phones, computers and the internet had not been invented. We did not have running water. We used kerosene lamps and candles for lighting and I went to bed early! We drew our

Find: kerosene lantern, basket, stone wall, bugle, car battery, happy people.

water from two stone lined, hand-dug wells, using buckets.

We had an old bathtub in the cottage but it took so long to bail enough water from the well and warm it up on a stove that we rarely used it to bathe! We used instead a "sun shower"—a black plastic

Find: Mattress, black tarp, motorcycle, black bag "sun shower," smiling girl finally clean!

bag fitted with a hose and shower head. We filled this contraption with water and laid it in the sunshine to warm. Worked like a charm!

We were led by a neighbor down a rough, shadowy dirt road to find a small shack that had once been a home. There we obtained a very small but sound wood burning cook stove. We bought an old upright wood burner for heating purposes.

I remember well the first few nights under our newly installed tin roof— lying in sleeping bags on the floor. Snow flakes drifted from above, coming through the cracks of our rough sawn siding on the eaves. We'd finished just in the nick of time!

We had been very fortunate to buy our

54 acres for only $13,000! But little did we know that deep in an overgrown gully on the property lay the rusting

A car frame, a white car roof, an old fashioned washer, a mower blade for a tractor. Not junk:the frame of a barn roof in the background; a man

carcasses of a dozen junked cars! Frames, axles, dashboards—everything but the engines! At one point, we had them pulled out of thegully but it took years to find someone to   haul them away. What a day for celebration that was!

And there was so much building to do! We converted a dilapidated shack into a firewood shed/garage. And another collapsing ramshackle structure became a chicken shed to house the dozen Rhode Island Reds that we'd brought from Pennsylvania. And we also built a barn.

Larry's parents who lived in Pennsylvania, had been farmers who were getting on in years and they owned an old post and beam barn which had been hit by a car and never repaired. They generously gave us the barn which we tore down and hauled to West Virginia. Some fiasco that was! Our $400 flatbed from 1950 (?) broke down halfway home. But not to worry. It broke down right in front of a commercial garage. We called one of our kind new West Virginia neighbors who came to fetch us home. And the mechanic at the garage fixed that old

Find: Boss talking to worker about how to do a better job laying the stones of a barn foundation.

clunker and the barn was delivered.

All that remained was to build it and you can see it in some of our photos. Larry, God Bless Him, had to cut mostly all new mortis and tenon joints!

Then what? The "hollow" where we lived was deep between two ridges. The sun rose there at about 10 am and set at 4 pm in the winter. We decided we needed more sunshine. We envisioned solar heating and wind turbines and

Find: Girl with a hammer, cement blocks; one of the posts.

such. And the logical next step was to build a family-sized house up on the hillside on the sunny side of the hollow. So we did it.

Thus the story, of course, goes on and

Find: Bean poles, girl catching white cabbage butterflies; cat (Good luck with finding the cat!)

on! I have so many sweet, wistful memories that feature a backdrop of seasons and forests and beautiful skies, new mowed hay, stocking up firewood and fresh home made bread.

Alas, although we pondered ways to earn income from the land, my husband eventually decided to go back to teaching and coaching. He was good at it! And I homeschooled my two sons. Indeed, there is nothing like sitting before a fireplace and reading "The Lion, The Witch and The Wardrobe" to a child!

BUT "WHY?" You might ask; "WHY" would anyone do as we did? And that's a very important question with a plethora of answers. !!!

But to keep it simple...Both my husband and I were very "spiritual" people. I had "majored" in the study of religions in college, including Eastern and Western traditions, mythology, and the psychology of religion. Larry read the Bible 37 times in his lifetime and never lost his enthusiasm.

We definitely differed in our spiritual particulars. WE DID NOT ALWAYS AGREE! BUT one thing that WE DID AGREE upon was the Sacredness of all Nature and the Mother Earth. It is, in fact, the common Ground upon which humans all walk. Modern life, we believed, distances humanity from that which many call "The Source" or "God" or "Great Spirit" and so on. And modern life tends to deceive us into believing that we can not be happy without so many things that we'd actually do better without!

We had lots of friends who believed similarly. We were called "Hippies" or

The Stone Cottage, smoke, the finished barn in the background, snowy hillside; All Good Things!

"Transplants" or just "Back to the Landers."

Humanity must realize that Nature is one of the primary keys to our health, happiness and evolutionary destiny. To quote John Muir, "Everybody needs beauty as well as bread, places to play and pray in, where Nature may heal and give strength to body and soul."

My husband Larry wrote a poem for our wedding ceremony which beautifully expresses his particular "take" on his Love of and Faith in the Natural world.

I will share it with you now.

Union with Nature

Before creation, naught had stirred;
Then God spoke forth His Holy word;
And worlds responded, The cosmos heard;
It felt His mighty hand.

He formed the breadth and depth of space;
Paths of planet, the starry trace;
This world of ours fell into place;
The seas, the sky, the land.

And when all finally came to rest;
The Lord was pleased, and man was blessed;
In nature God is manifest;
To those who are aware.

Woodland and meadow sing glad refrain;
Seasons emerge and seasons wane;
Nature's mysteries themselves explain;
To those who truly care.

To nature the two of us shall go;
To work, to worship, learn and grow;
And reap the bounty it may bestow;
Upon us, day by day.

Betsy & Larry

"Unite with Nature" noble theme;
That dreamers hold in high esteem;
It's here we've gone to find that dream;
And here we plan to stay.

It's here in nature we have planned;
To have our life and love expand;
To love each other and the land;
Our intimate desire.

God grant us then that we endure;
That we may live both hard and sure;
And if we're worthy-if we're pure;
That others we inspire.

So God when He the soil did sift;
The hollows carve, the mountains lift;
Made nature then His greatest gift;
The finest He could give.

No finer place to work the loam;
To have our children freely roam;
No finer place to have our home;
No finer place to live.

There's no place like Homespun, one project after another....

About the Author:
Elizabeth Richie aka "Spring Frog"

I grew up running free, playing in the lush forests, cornfields and meadows of the Susquehanna River Valley of central Pennsylvania. One of my favorite haunts was "The Swamp" where catching (and releasing) frogs, climbing trees, and building forts with the neighborhood "gang" was often the order of the day. My elementary school was within walking distance and each day when I passed my grandfather's house on the way to school, I waved to him as he stood waiting at his living room window. I was blessed to be raised in a happy home.

I hold a 1975 BA from Princeton University, Dept. of Religion. This was the road less traveled! I studied both Eastern and Western traditions, the psychology of religions, mythology, and anthropology. I discovered Rudolf Steiner's Anthroposophy which awakened me to the powerful notion that humanity is in the process of an amazing, ongoing spiritual evolution.

After academia, I did a stint as a news reporter and then I went off with my Beloved to West Virginia—as **Homespun: A Return to the Land**, describes. We built a fine house on the hillside and had wonderful years together raising our two sons.

At one point, I became obsessed with finding a Native American Medicine Woman to teach me. I found her as a speaker at an interfaith conference held at the Krisna community located near Moundsville WV. She is a remarkable, magical woman who was raised by her grandmother in the Smoky Mountains of North Carolina.

I am very open minded and open hearted when it comes to spirituality, as long as it is rooted in love and respect. I am also very curious in regard to the phenomena of so-called "ET's" and their role in human life.

In 2008, I returned to Pennsylvania to care for my parents. And the adventure of life continues unabated!

I very much appreciate that you've decided to read **Homespun: A Return to the Land**

I am also the author of the book, **The Whole Kit and Caboodle Is...As Sacred As 1,2,3**. It's available through my website, *https://sacredas123.com*, Amazon, and other fine booksellers. To find it, use the whole title and my Medicine Name in Cherokee, Du'Tsu, which means "Spring Frog."

As humanity evolves -- pulling itself up by its own flimsy bootstraps --- the People's true destiny awakens. It can be no other way. Sinner, Saint or Shaman, Christian, Muslim, Hindu, Jewish, Buddhist, Agnostic, Atheist, Voodoo Economist --- Your True Nature is Divinity! So says Spirit Divine in The Whole Kit and Caboodle Is... As Sacred As 1,2,3! Humanity has a Covenant to keep. The Creator that has revealed this Covenant-in the mathematical concepts of The One, The Two, and The Three, in the Circle and the Spiral, and in the Giving of All Gifts-speaks the Words, "I Am," from every quarter. The Co-Creators called "Humans" must pledge their Truth, their "Treowth" to that same covenant, the universal Covenant of Love!